Acquist by Elizabeth Sewell

Typeset in 10 point Palacio (Compugraphic) by
Allied Photocomp Systems, Inc., Durham, North Carolina.

Our Culture Compared to a Glass of Champagne

    And up the bubbles go
    Swiftly, whizzing past us, burbling
    "Success" sibilant and swoop!
      Rush to the golden surface, burst
        Into nonentity   but oh
          The dearest spirits sink, heavy and slow,
            Drawn downwards   drownwards   dregwards
          To a slew of
            Darkness, all my loves, last and first,
            And I too of
              Never   that effervescent class
              Prickling through our liquid medium
                So up   so down   so upsidedown   and so
              Where I made one, turn down an empty glass. . .

Signor of the images:

That there echo
laughter's high purport here,
confident and remote
as branch of flowering dogwood carried
to triumph through the doorways.

Prayer for a Friend's House

> . . .*il signor di quelli imagini.* . .
> Giordano Bruno

Signor of the images:

That there be,
as elder custom was,
sweet rushes underfoot
for springing instep
and gathered up, timely, thrown out
with apple-peel, feathers, crusts of bread,
and new green strewn.

Signor of the images:

That there be
cold airs and warm,
passages, lingerings, the scent
of lilac, woodsmoke,
of oil and rosemary in the pot
for sharp-set kin.

Signor of the images:

That there be
small shadow-cells of mind
in whose cool hexagons
bee-thoughts take shape
for roseate voyages.

Lamplight and friendship, eiderdown for cosy,
Shutters set to, and heart set open wide,
Sleep folding petals' silk and the soul's powers.
How maybug entered here I can't decide.
His trouble was, decoyed perhaps by flowers,
He had crept somehow from his world to ours.
I pulled the shutters back, threw up the sash
(Can buzzing in my hand) and in a flash
I saw the maybug's world, the other side.

Twined roseleaf garlands thicketed the sill
Across the golden stone, around the bars,
The valley liquefying into stars,
Charged with warm blue of early night, a still
In which was crushed the honeysuckle's comb
And candid lilacs frothing down the hill
To melt the spirit in a kiss of foam.
I held my breath – but he was quite at home.
I emptied out the can and heard him drop
Onto the still-warm ledge, a solid plop,
Then closed the sash and left him to his will.

Now, laid in bed, my mind is still aware
Of that small scarab busy at his games,
Chasing through clematis shocks his lusty dames,
His sable silvered by the stars' soft flare,
Eyebrows a-semaphore to every breeze.
But then I think, suppose that I and Clare
Were in his world, we might be ill at ease,
And blinded by Betelgeuse and high Altair,
Fall in Aquarius' pot behind the trees,
And Someone, much amazed to find us there,
Would see us ignominiously returned
To where our own small bedside tapers burned,
And we would pause, and stumble into sleep
As I do now, a quietude as deep,
Blue, and impartial, as the summer air.

Maybug in the Cotswolds

Bzz..zz! it went, a small metallic blare
In the far corner by the window-sill.
The ear locates a noise with pointed skill:
"I think you've got a maybug over there."
Heads cocked, we listened, smiling; then I said,
"It's in your watering-can!" Sceptical, Clare
Went to her bath. I, perching on the bed,
Began to fill the crossword in (in red).
Bzz..zz again, this time an S.O.S.
Of angry impotence or just distress.
I tiptoed over with a cautious stare.

It's odd perhaps to find a watering can,
Small, green, self-satisfied with lifted nose,
Gracing so fair a bedroom, but Clare grows
Rose-pink geraniums in that sunny span,
And it's a great deal odder to have found
A maybug in it, obviously *en panne*.
The pot had one small opening, through whose round
I peered for fear the creature might be drowned,
But rust had worked the surface tanned and dried,
And sure enough the maybug *was* inside,
Fat, furry, alien as Caliban.

He was exploring, in a pensive crawl,
The metal O where he had come to grief,
But muddled by a dead geranium leaf
Which also sought that opening in its fall.
Curious, I thought, the pot should hold so much —
A water-can for grave, a leaf for pall —
No death for maybug, though; I'm scared of such,
But then his eyebrows' tuftiness must touch
The heart, small hands thumb-tilted in derision;
One thing seemed plain — our absolute division;
And then I saw the meaning in it all.

There are two window-worlds the panes divide.
I knew ours well, chintz curtains blue and rosy,

For a Friend's Forthcoming Marriage

Through the wilderness
        through waters
Where the small green leaves shake
   and you must find their meaning
Through gold light
       and thorns
Past the basketwork dishes of parched grain and the rosy fruits
        mango   plum   pomegranate
   offered and accepted
Among cities of blood and iron
       through ruin
Gate after gate   pillar by pillar
Through hangings   heavy cream linen   that breathe and sway
   on their jasper hooks
      To the vision
   with us all   with us all

Lines to a Large Sculptured Head in a University Library

This individual's head is split:
He does not seem aware of it,
But with a vacant gaze and bland
Daily observes the scurrying band
Of those who follow learning's call,
Up, down, across this marble hall,
With dull demeanour, nervous tread,
And, frequently, a splitting head.

O were they thoughtless or malign
Who put him here? – so clear a sign
Or simulacrum of our fate,
Who started whole but learned too late
That we must also entertain
These glaring fissures of the brain.
We name thee, noble artifact,
The Academic – once intact
And now most absolutely cracked.

At a Conference of Humanistic Psychologists, the Lecturer happening to use the word *scribe*

THOTH, fair god of scribes
Under the copper sun
Compact, lithe, inscrutable,
The dust rises again
Round your clawed feet,
Dust of verbiage
Pulverous, caking *ennui*,
Grains of suffering.

Stroke me with a feather, fair god.
Nibble my right ear-lobe
With that huge beak (gently, please!)
Wink at me your membrane eyelid.
Bring us, sweetheart, soon, or I am going to die,
To green shades, to water.

Humanities Conference, Columbia University, May 10, 1974

We sit   white mandarins
In the towering parapet
  and the rain

Clothe us with huge stiff robes
Some of us with slender black mustachios
All of us with smooth round hats
To crown our gold-tinged Manchu faces

What wisdom   shall we speak
As we sit   straight-spined   noble
Elders aloft in our well-ventilated
  mausoleum?

Ah friend   build us poems!
Imagine clocks and wheels
The stubborn rising of the sun on Salisbury plain
Be architect   archangel   archeologist!
    We covet shelter
Scattered as we are   in the deserts
    of our disconnected lives.

Ellen Pollak

There was the smell of panic
two-hundred refugee palms and the prayer quite done
seeking solace in pockets   pressing on keys or change
lying sullen in laps
some tactfully covering mouths
or supporting chins laden with the heaviness of good-bye.
That was our first taste of dissolution,
of the bus-ride out,
of a hundred thousand wheels beginning to turn.

By a lake   under the sun
In the cold November air
For a very short moment
We stood like Adam on the mount of Vision
And, guided by your voice, viewed together
Past and future   imagined monuments of ages
          and horrors to come.

With the smooth oval   blue-grey stones
          of that narrow beach
I built   as in a broad flat plain
Ten Sarsen pillars in the sand
Across their tops five horizontal pieces lightly laid
No permanence of mortice or of tenon, lock or joint
No labor of mass effort   but of solitary care.

Yet in my dreams now   leaning
  my whole weight   arms front
pushing against the inside of a massive concrete wall
I tremble
No one of us is Samson
In our pedantic darknesses the Philistian temples will not fall
though trilithons of Druid worship tumbled over centuries
          ago.

Oasis in Zion

> O for life's sake, my neighbour,
> Hold up your spread hand, lay palm to mine
> though glass be cold between
>   There is love, focus it as in a burning-glass
> hand to my hand
>   From *Danforth Conference* by Elizabeth Sewell

"I wish I had eight hands," you said,
But I saw at least a hundred
Each of us holding a palm to one of yours
In an attitude of universal prayer
As we stood in that same large room
Not held in check by glass this time
But forming a magnificent whole.

One huge still wheel
With spokes of human flesh
Not moving, but eternal
Not attached to any cart
Nor any chariot in the sky
Not created or invented
But ourselves.

You were the hub   a pillar
   enabling us to lean
   to stare down through the interstices of bodies
   onto the floor of the cave   into the abyss.
   You showed us ruins   but gave us words
   that choreographed our souls
   and bade us dream.
Our thirsty hearts grew full
   and we nodded
   drunken humility.

What a terrible moment it was when the first hand fell
   that broke our clear circumference!

Take one another with us on our pilgrimage
    As I take you.

[The poem above elicited a poem as response from one of the members of the Conference, Ellen Pollak. It is, by permission, included here on the following page.]

Danforth Conference. Zion, Illinois. November, 1974

Here was a ballroom
        high   cold   empty
Yet we did no dancing
There were walls of glass
Appeared and slid around us
Bent and slid around us
Bent again angle by angle
Singled and squared us in
      Iced bees in an invisible comb
          some pinned tight with arms over their heads
          some pounding, some yelling, some with cold tears
                    dripping
    as we went about our verbal hustings
      ate our meals   attended the requisition business
noise of tongues   rising to crash and roar
but no crack in our cells
suffocation that blue lake vistas could not palliate
      nor the heaving up before us of huge issues
      global moralities and disasters

O for life's sake, my neighbour,
Hold up your spread hand, lay palm to mine
though glass be cold between
      There is love, focus it as in a burning-glass
hand to my hand
Differ, dislike, reject as you will, no matter
In each of us remember the solar fire
Sun will flare at this intentional touch
      For "palm to palm is holy palmer's kiss"
      as another voice says

      Palmers and pilgrims
      Shall we come out, go free,
Put on your sun- and moon-masks
Mask of lion and ibex and horned owl and newborn child

To Accompany a Proposal for a Conference

The great waves are upon us,
A sea, surrealist,
Of human faces innumerable rising
And the breakers smash our rocky concrete
With the sea-smoke curling backwards —
O salt smoke and acrid in the dull roar of dreams!

So stand, nose to wind,
Snuffing wary, animal-like,
True friend from foe, and beyond that
To learn to follow down the moment's air
Earth under rain for the rice-planting,
Warm human flesh, lips laid upon it,
And long-forgotten flowers.

Thurs-day

In regard to this listening for the gods' language:

Two days ago they spoke hippopotamus rain,
Huge mirrors clashed together like cymbals,
Shivering into white spikes,
Prodigious bumps and bangs;

Yesterday grey and still
They spoke the catbird long alighted
    on the dead bough;

Today the wor(l)d is gamesome,
A little wandering witty wind do they utter,
The fainting of dawn-pink Rose of Sharon bloom
    onto flat rock;

Or, read the other way,
Menace is that rose-fall
(Remember the terrible dawn dream of imminent slaughter?)
    grey is grey still,
    and Tuesday nothing but horse-play, my dear.

For Giambattista Vico and the Others with Him

Can he himself make new
   Move into darkness
   Slough off the mortal image, re-emerge
   In starlight only —
   This, like mating,
   No work for the day —
      Without invitation or return to chaos
      Voluntary anarchy
      Which is for weaklings and the sophisticated-obtuse
Can he himself make new
   Sleek as a snake
   Glossed black and silver
A hero forces the very gods to change.

   Then shall he hear
   The great ranks go by,
   Hosts of the air
   Shifting in measure
      Not for them the agony, cold sweats, abandonments
      Of our thinking substance
   Shall the hero see
   Dull glint of swords
   Slope high down the darkness,
   Our archangelic powers, mail on thigh,
      And beyond, the changeless bright geometry of the stars
      Which need not think and alter

Scion, and rare, in this line
   Frustrate, ailing, misconstered
   At peril, darkly glorious
Set out
   Coolly possessed of faculties
   In full attention
Set out, hero-making-other, to divine.

Of Power

Happy those unsolicited
By the gods;
They walk abroad
In orchard and paddock,
Stirring only the grass-clumps,
Duly to follow
Quotidian paths.

Nor theirs (happy!)
The shining presences,
Tall as young trees,
Bright clouds, marble,
Appearing unwonted
On grove's edge,
On livingroom wall,
To pose demands.

For Giordano Bruno. February 17th

Did they cast your terrible horoscope,
  dear Master?
Oh I can transmute these elements
  send you upwards
  in fire and flowers towards stars bright enough
  to pierce the morning

not so

If I am to serve you
  am not to betray
  those slow dawn hours of prime and matins
  after those slow dungeon years
  no cloak no pillow no books almost no food
  but today, anno domini sixteen hundred,
  led out
  in your early fifties
  out into the packed Campo de' Fiori
  out, your intention, filial, toward the Sun,
  out of this world

naked, gagged, roped,
you could still move your head,
turn away your dark Nolan eyes,
like the last gesture of a woman before rape,
from the brandished image of a younger Death
they shook in front of your nose
like a fist

crowd rumour, or silence
greasy smoke thick up into
the mild Roman sky

and you already dead by now

May I love and serve you

May I know you better

Figures on a Magical Ground

These appear first
Throbbing inside your temples
Formalized star or lily
Light-pulsing diagrams
Arc, line, pentacle

These others ribbon out,
Run, lobed and sinuous,
Black against sea-burned emerald

Or gold
Cuneiform, darts and arrows
Flung high in sooty nimbus
As arms embattled
Field sable, fretted or,

Some mere outlines
Some fully shadowed in
Move, starry and beckoning,
On our limitless dancing-floor

Runes

By the great mercies
I have been returned
To the sources of power
To live thereby
The flames dancing on their bed of coals
The water jetting from its hole in the rock
Alive the elements
And we
Neither soused nor burned
By the great mercies
Have returned

II

Where our eyes met
Was, leaf-drowned, root-locked,
The wood well,
Hazel, green green willow,
Quiet as liquid sky

But look – the centre –
What sent one hoop of ripple
To our feet?
Grayling, goldfish? – or dropped from above
Amulet, tiny stone idol
From the clouds

Do not stir
In such strong magic:
Scarcely breathe:
Scan only the fretted resonances
Shivering now the surface

This well is fathomless

Circle/Net

Exercise to break thought patterns out of linearity

I

Fisher Sun,
Fling wide your fiery net
This break of day
> We slippery Pisces-fish
> Will dance, evade the flap
> Of your weighted fanning out
> On our water surface
> Yet shooting in our play
> Into your web
> At last
Draw us to you —
Round up our knotted circle
Towards lovingdarkness
At day's close

Kind

When they came upon it,
>amazement: were those not all gone,
long ago, those monster saurians, rattling scales,
>mere tribal memory.

The hugeness stunned: a long low hill
contoured to the grass and dust
over which the wind whistled.

It simply lay.

When once they realized it was not quite dead,
>standing around, whispering suddenly, foolishly,
>in the bright air,
>jerking back at its occasional twitches,
did sharp compassion goad them into a straggled chain
of pygmies running to and fro to the women,
tempting it with the bitter wild lettuce and dark hedge fruits
>of their own eating,
>and in the end, desperately,
spooning pannikins of warmed milk down the tunnel throat
>until it died.

Or did they exult, such things were now no moe,
leapt with brave cries over its sprung rib-cage
>dunes and hummocks,
taught their profuse small children to do the same
until the enormous body split at last
>and engulfed them all.

III

Watchman, what of the Night?

As I opened the door, one vineleaf fell;
    Curled rattling shell –
They are ploughing over the hill tonight
    In near-full dark, and all seemed well,
No threat implied in the distant light
    Of a star or two, but just the same,
As I opened the door one vineleaf fell,
And it seemed that little thud could tell
    Finality to all that frame,
        To wight, to flame –
Come in: doors tight: shake off that spell.
What of the night? One vineleaf fell.

II

After reversal,
Wait the arriving:
    Down dew-dazzled hillside,
    Where ant column marches,
    Past red oleanders:
By the paths of dispersal
Comes Love's reviving.

After derangement,
Turn to the centre:
    Under starlight or thunder,
    To his courts in the morning,
    In power of scirocco:
By the doors of estrangement
Love will re-enter.

Whose sweetness must distract.
See now more wholly apt,
Francesco limps in rags,
Hangs Benedetto, rapt,
On Subiaco crags.

Three from Boccea, Italy

I

Kennst du das Land...

Dream not the olive's fat
Drops benison to the dust
Or vines bestow their must
On any but the vat.
Here the unfriended ground
Gold-purple thistle pranks,
And arid lizards pound
Lozenge-striated flanks.

Here umber ploughlands trudge
Devoid of tenderness,
And in blue heaven's largesse
The beasts, the women drudge.
Here birds are daily shot
Out of the scented pines.
On the hard skyrim squat
The steel-blue Apennines.

Meet, then, to meet it here:
The overflowing, whole,
The heartfelt, anxious, sole,
Deep, tender, none more near,
The sealed with self, the sheer
Longdrawn — and long ignored
Immeasurably dear
Lovelonging of my Lord.

Not in a greener tract
Where nature can respond;
Least in a lover's bond

VII

**For a University President's, and dear friend's, demission.
Mid-December.**

No need to go into the night: the night is upon us.
Madness to think of spring, tonight, if ever.
Somewhere a house burns suddenly and falls inward.
Over the iron city an arctic wind.

A random shot and a child or a great one finished.
God's in suburbia attending a Christmas party.
His minions exact the uttermost farthing for folly.
Over the iron city an arctic wind.

The stars burn holes in the man-hungry river.
A woman screams and runs. Ice on trees pendant.
Ice on the vocal chords. Sing softly, poet.
Over the iron city an arctic wind.

VI

The Change

> *After three thousands years of explosion. . .*
> *the Western world is imploding.*
>   Marshall McLuhan

We have imploded
Into ourselves
Into darkness
Into one another
The hearts and failings
The labyrinth
Into the shell
The grand conch of time
Into the deep sea
With the salt taste of blood in the mouth
Six miles down
Pressure of tons to the square inch
Search for us by echo-sounder
Ask us nothing
Do not draw us up in the Agassiz trawl of your mind
Or we shall burst
Surfacing only as fragments
Delicate jawbone set with needle-sharp teeth
Entrails
A huge black eye
And will tell you nothing
Of time compressed into water dense as blood
Of hearts and failings in fathomless transformation
Of life beginning

V

For Doves and Hawks

There will not be safe ground under the feet
   Ever again,
Even the feet change,
Learn the feel of a branch beneath them,
Grow grasping claws, nervous rounded grip,
   In the great winds coming.

There will not be sure hold for the heart,
So many left downwind far behind,
   The downy breast and nesting
Now only the loving tenderness of the young
Given and received, and likely brief
   In this fierce weather.

   And the hands,
Are they become wings? – then for covering
What heads they can, where they can,
Or to plane at a certain height,
The speeded bird-pulse throbbing the life away,
   And cry the battle.

IV

"How it strikes a contemporary" —
Sunday morning.

Browning on poet's task: observe, collect the news,
    And then retell it to "Our Lord the King"
      By verbal relation.
Today it suddenly dawns
    My task is no such thing:
      I am the information.

But then: change, and exchange:
    Other such tasks (the Mass?) in turn defy
      One-way convention,
If to decentralized Power
    Crazed nervework that is I
      Is offered in reciprocal intention.

So here, this morning's missive, I wait to brief you
    With sense of desperate breakage or renewing
      As how it feels on earth

Should this be what in heaven you need to know —
    I merely mention, body, it, scarce-known Our Lord the King,
      For what it's worth.

III

"My tired strength" — as Serge Hughes translated *mia virtute stanca*

> Quali i fioretti, dal notturno gelo
> chinati e chiusi, poi che il sol li'mbianca,
> si drizzan tutti aperti in loro stelo:
> tal mi fec'io di mia virtute stanca. . .
>
> *Inferno*, Canto II, 127–30

If there is to be
No single loving vision
As too absorbing,
Nor dewfall by night
Nor the food of moon on leaves
As too disturbing,
There will be soft gleams
Here also, of a sudden,
As the sight of one dear man,
As a kiss of peace from two others,
Is a trope of heaven,
As in a late dream
One second of imageless hope
Rainbowed the waking,
And innocent flowerbell or spirits shaken and fearful
Lift as if summoned:
        Continue then:
        Offer the tired strength:
        We will make that journey.

II

What God Suffers

What god suffers
In this shrunk frame
Unreasonable weeks and months long

Here was no triumphant creature
Wound in grapevines
As the dolphins leaped and sprayed
Here no defier
Teeth set against vultures
Ready, ever-renewing, to endure

Only self-resurrecting fear
Which transforms nothing
And, buried, rots, not grows

But a shabby rib-cage lolled
Along the mountains, used up
By nothing live, rain, wind

What suffers by its nature clogs the tongue
The god, the ruined titan,
The very young.

Complaining like a creaking door
Je n'ai pas de plume,
Je suis dans mon lit,
Except that there is no bed
And no house
And only very few words left
And little time even for those few such as
"Help" and "friend"
Pour l'amour de Dieu.

And I dare not again live in them,
The great dream-houses,
Knowing them smoke and illusion
Though I might visit you all some time
And with envy.
Ouvre-moi ta porte
But come out, you also,
We could sit in the gutter together
Au clair de la lune
And talk at last, if we were to hold one another's hand,
Of the remaining solidity of the human body
And the human soul,
And we could pray and learn again some taste of faith and hope
In impossible wilderness
Au clair de la lune
As the great grey dream-mansions tatter and shred in the moonlit
                                                                  wind
And see what to do next
Pour l'amour de Dieu.

The Bensalem Poems

The following group of seven poems came out of the experience of founding and chairing Bensalem, the Experimental College at Fordham University. The first six poems were presented as the "Dean's Report" on our first year of working, and were accepted as such.

I

Au Clair de la Lune

Au clair de la lune
Mon ami – you inside there
In that grey so solid-seeming house
Where I also used to live,
The moon comes through the towers of smoke
That shift and sway uneasily in this wilderness –
Can you hear me at all?

Prête-moi ta plume
Older and wiser friend
Pour écrire un mot
Because it is hard to get across to you,
You behind those smoky fog-dream walls,
What has happened:

That the houses only appear
But have gone,
And the schools and churches
And the law courts and public buildings,
Only their smoke-mansions pillar up
Au clair de la lune
As I sit in the gutter
And hear a voice that is possibly yours

II

will and goodwill are lost
    in the deep woods

the compass, friends — now why is it
    pointing in all directions

forest roof overhead too thick
    for sun or star

only our own blanched faces mooning here, there, yonder,
    must draw us together

Charm against Anxiety

I

Rustle the family longevity-robes
Out of the cedar press

Let them be steeped in palm oil,
Wine, a slight tincture
Of crushed peach kernels

Swathe their warm silk firmly around limb and torso
That the skin cohere
With the blue dragons, gold chrysanthemums

That limits be set,
The vital spirits transpire no more
Through porous nerve endings

That there be bounds, bonds, formed, perceptible,
Within which to shape the visceral body,
Against which to sleep.

More than One Thing

Given my split self
This dry age would word me

    Clinical diagnoses

So would not I; let me but grope
Old forms, own forms, to solve

    Perceived soul-data

Such the twin sphere-line,
Day/Night that skims the globe's blue,

    Alternating eternally

Such the Olmec mask
Fused in carved stone the gash
Of jaguar snarl with sobbing babe,

    Lachrymae rerum. . .

The first, a life-pulse;
The next, their old saws tell,
Mystery — a rain god —

    Fruit-bringing, propitious

Dream before Winter

O my October riddle, sing to me
In the nights when, sleepless,
    wind blows and rain

Where is the true treasure?
                      came
out of a dream, Monday, a morning,
And I search now hereabouts
    under the dead leaves,
Turning over their sodden gold,
Catch the late birds' piping:

Death clues me first, and after,
    beauty? truth?
Buckle on winter shoes, set out for where,
    the any where,
Where happy, happy, the absolute seeds
    lurk warmly fulvous,
    by day, by dark glowing,
Wait to be manifest.

Attack

For the fourth time
In this my livelong day
The human voices have at my centre:
The cry – "Disfigured!"
The "I recoil!"
They cry for change, conversion

They, they, they, they

Enough,
I pray

Let me be God's monster
If so I may.

Separation

The dreadful clamour
ended
gives place
to silence so extreme
I must take its quality
with the small tuning-fork I hold
in my right hand.

New Year Resolutions

I will drain
long draughts of quiet
as a purgation;

remember
twice daily
who I am;

will lie o'nights
in the bony arms
of Reality and be comforted.

III

When you tell me of my "deep wisdom",
Having set me before myself
As deeply blind,
I say to you, "My soul,
You are talking through your hat"

Perhaps both our souls
Should put on their funny hats
And talk to one another

    The hats would nod

        Like mountains
        Like weathercocks
        Like harebells in the wind

each in other, where we rest
not wilful or possest,
striving nevertheless
for something of that lovely artifice
in frost and fire.

to which end,
o lay your Form on mine,
memory, presence, what's to come;
our stream runs forward,
and singing out of human wretchedness
to love itself
we offer that desire.

II

Au Bois Dormant

Within a thorn circle
My love lies

Enclosed there, he my heart, darkness
Towering above him

Have I sown this darkness, exhaled
This quickset hedge?

There were old tales would tell, but they
Are long forgotten

Wide-eyed, scanning the plain that holds us both,
I hear

My love cry out in his sleep — "see
What magic has done"

in answer to your letter

I

each living thing
sends rays, behind, before;
the backward, memory;
ahead, its prophecy.

such Forms
impinge in friendship, overlap,
field on magnetic field,
or hand laid upon hand,
the fingers pointing true;
but we have gone beyond,
married our two,
intense the Forms, the figure
not yet right —
o is it congruence of living triangles,
or parallels of light?

we share our pasts
though not their sum; similarly
some presentness.

strong runs, to me, my forward line
and clear to sight;
your wedded Form too often turbid opalline,
and I have asked forgiveness
who thought it cloud of yours, not cataract
of these own eyn.

one built a pleasure-dome
of such impalpable stuff, his sun and ice,
yet all unmoving for our life
a figure, where we would stream

Discouragement

I'll walk no more those lovely lanes,
Where hazel-knop and withy plait
A wreathed green traverse,
And the sun strikes hot.

I will not go where creepers twine
Their supple stems, and flower
The endless on and on,
Since now you never meet me there.

I will forget them, leaf by leaf,
Calyx and cusp, silk-haired, forget
The veins drawn white in emphasis,
Down to the last detail,
And all be dust and weariness.

Nights when we lie alone
Or are together laid
Can only modulate,
The range being infinite,
Not alter or suppress
The murmurs of the heart,
As instant as the pulse,
As thought resonates thought,
As set of star to star,
When we are all the worlds'
And all our own.

Cor ad Cor Loquitur

Nights when I lie alone
I hold long talks with you
At three or four o'clock,
Of the day's enterprise,
Of what a dream imparts,
Articulate interchange
That goes on all the time,
Workaday, say, in kitchens,
Or late and long some evenings
Over the telephone.

Nights when we lie alone
We may be side by side
Yet for shared weariness
Will make a tacit space
And in that depth of sleep
May touch or hold a hand
Twice, three times in the hours
Of silence no less filled
With love's shy courtesy,
Arcane a chaperone.

Nights when we lie alone
Are in no way estranged
From those of making love,
The closest conversation
Of nerve-nets fleshed and housed
By spirits at their play,
Till head at rest by head
Rings still as skies that orb
Their rolling organ-music
Our senses must scale down
And seem at times to have caught
At point of sleep some one
Last perfect semitone.

A Figure: for the Making of Love

                            and gold
                two hands   and wine
                      only it is dark
                and where: soft flame, the lamp
             brown, boat-shaped, stutters at the wick,
        our two small mediterranean bodies, by what shores
                   this chamber, cave, tomb,
                      minoan or mycenean
                       tholos honeycomb
                    of sweetness and of death

the hands are ours
mysterious twins laid palm to palm
as we have often matched them
in love and quiet

the gold is clearer,
massy, a ring, braided gold beaten,
neither hand wears it
it is simply there

the wine, suspended,
hangs dense and heavy in the cup
from vineyards sloping
into god-troubled seas

      unpossessed gifts   hands, lips, yours, mine
                   offered between

How, for love, no poem will do

No image serves
For this at-oneness,
Not even the figure
Of bodies loving,
No tendril of vines
How twined so ever,
Nor fish, suspense
Twin and all-touching,
Gravityless
In greensilk flood

> *were I watersmeet*
> *or woman with child*
> *or that child itself*
> *might I say what I mean*

As longboat cradles
Its form in air,
As object to shadow
When sun not shines,
As sap and fibre
The mutual flesh,
Bride and groom,
Bathe and embroider –
   With hint of between,
   No image serves

> *were I watersmeet*
> *or woman with child*
> *or that child itself*
> *might I say what I mean*

The Small Hours

                O let him sleep
    Naked and young, gone sweetly far away,
          Call him not back to you.
          He has done all during the day
              God asked him do.
              O let him sleep.
Send out your self, being too fearful to dress and creep
Around this black city of the heart you have brought us to:
Your thoughts can go stumble about out there in the grey
Between night and morning. Others who stray,
Reckless in heat or misery, turning a corner, may
         Counter, sudden, in alien interview
            Those ghosts he cannot lay.
Let him sleep on, lovely, untouched, this long night through.

The Good Day

If one could have the choosing, this would be
A good day to die,
The city quiet, a brief wind about the streets,
Light neutral and dry,
The little rivers of physical pain down the breastbone probably
meaningless,
Unlikely an alibi.

Not, of all things, the burden of youth's tenderness
To take up afresh,
Not to admit once more the absolute spell and vulnerability
Flesh lays, sweetly, to flesh,
Not to undergo the total change all sexual encounter, however
tentative, brings with it,
(O changed the earth and sky!)
Given the choice – we are not – this would be
A good day to die.

And those who plunge headlong into never-ending storms,
Yet fixed and steady stands the immortal heart.

Yet woe betide me, if from. . .

And were I straight to say,
Here have I come to gaze on the Heavenly Ones,
They, they themselves, would cast me down lower than any living,
The false priest into nether darkness, that there I might sing
The warning song for those who have ears to hear.

From Hölderlin's fragment, *The Fire from Heaven*

As on holyday, when the countryman walks abroad
To take a morning look at the fields,
Came down the cooling sheets of lightning all the hot night long,
And thunder still rumbling in the distance,
And the stream is making its way back between its banks,
The ground all new and green,
The vines dripping with heaven's gladdening rain,
And the stand of trees rises up in the quiet sunshine:

So stand they, under and through the blessed storm,
So stand. . .
. . . .

And as in the eye there blazes a spark when such an one
Has taken on high resolve,
So now in souls of poets a sparkfire kindles,
New in its portent, calling to world-deeds,
And that which came earlier and was scarcely sensed, is now for the first time
Made manifest,
And those who turned the ploughlands with a smile for us
In servant guise, they are made known to thee,
The All-quickened, the powers of the very Gods. . .

So fell, as poets say, when she besought
To see God visibly, his lightning on Semele's house
And she, the divinely smitten, brought forth
The storm fruit, holiest Bacchus.
Therefrom the sons of earth drink in
The fire from heaven unattainted.
Yet it behoves us — and I speak to the poets — in the storms of God
To stand bareheaded to All-father's lightning stroke,
With own hand to seize it and then
Offer it, heavenly gift, to the people, husked in song.
For are we of innocent heart, like children,
Are we of unsmutched hands,
The Father's blaze in its incandescence makes scorch nor scar,
And stirred to the depths in pity at hero's pains,

So sang the Dark Sisters.
Hearkens those songs
The old one, the outcast
In cavernous darkness,
Broods on sons and sons' sons,
And shakes his head.

Song of the Fates from Goethe's *Iphigenie:*

The gods – best fear them,
You humankind!
They gripe allpower
With hands never slackening,
Turn it hither, thither,
As liketh them.

Fear them twice over,
Whome'er they uplift!
On peaks and cloud-cover
Are chairs set ready
Round golden tables.

Should brawling break out,
The guests pitch headlong,
Humbled and howled at,
Into gulfs of darkness
Where vainly they wait
Gloom-imprisoned
For judgment and justice.

But they, they abide
Eternally feasting
At golden tables.
They go stepping over
Summit to summit:
From crevice and chasm
Steams godwards the lifebreath
Of titans throttled,
Like whiffs of burnt offering,
A delicate vapour.

Lords and masters,
They avert from whole clans
Any glance of blessing,
Take pains not to see
In children's children
The still-speaking likeness
Of once loved forebear.

Rilke: the poem inscribed on his grave

O Rose, reiner Widerspruch, Lust,
Niemandes Schlaf zu sein unter so viel Lidern.

                Rose
               o you
              paradox
           pure and simple
           pleasing yourself
                to be
         under all those eyelids
             the sleep of
              no   one

Late Summer

    through the susurrus of this morning's heat,
    leafwash, bird-twitter, cicadas shrilling — Ears,
    best not miss that faint hiss on the wind:
        Atropos sharpens her shears.

Chance Meeting, Airport Motel Restaurant

It was the usual American desert
They call luxury,
Hot, dark, peopled with shadowy forms of men,
Power and no power, nor place for poet or woman or child,
Until you spoke and, one might say,
Nothing changed — except
        There were azaleas

Profusion, bounty, they rose whole glades and hillsides,
Coral, rust, pale gold, flamingo, plum and cherry,
Apricot, cream, the white of lilies and bread, blood-scarlet,
How could they come there, patiently waiting to be seen,
"Dreaming", in that strange Shelleyan phrase,
"Like a love-adept" — ?
        There were azaleas

A child could have gathered armfuls of them,
Blossoms massing like sunset clouds,
Faintly scented,
Fed with cold spring-water, touched by dew,
Their golden throats crying, to humans, poems,
Or promises made and kept —
        There were azaleas

And so much beauty one held one's head a moment,
Dizzy with vision,
Alone in the silent room
Before one slept —
        I remember azaleas
        And that you wept

And leant
The other way, so they must clutch
At seeming trivia, cup and plate and touch
Where suddenly itself would superimpose
The reflex of His care

And sent
Strange blessings of enormous tenderness
In the lost corners of the wilderness
Where love was simple as a rose
And all the spice-trees blossomed on the air

Mississippi Revisited

I

They saw what they went to see
   and something more,
It was the bony worked faces and the luminous eyes,
It was wrecked cabins still inhabited,
It was honeysuckle wafting all over
   and what else it was
They could hardly say
Except that it was painful as young black voices
   singing the National Anthem,
   and sharp as sudden death,
It was love and a different way.
It was mornings grey and heavy with Gulf steam,
It was tiny children being taught their letters
   in a corner of noise and dust,
It was poor and simple as the washed-out petticoat showing
   under a small girl's skirt,
It was a three nights' dream,
It was ultimate trust.
It was roses huge and yellow as moons
   sagging over the hedges,
It was the condemned school diningroom,
   a child's toes through her shoes,
It was shrill sweet birds' cries piercing the roar of speed
   as they and the landscape flew,
   uttering what, they could not understand,
It was, they think however, something about God,
   wholly unmanageable, absolutely new.

II

And went
A long way off to recoup His glory, find
Refreshment in dark fountains of His mind
And a benign absence might disclose
To them recovered prayer

Watching New York

Old, fat, ugly and incompetent,
Thirty-third, I, in line to the sullen cashier
Pre-Fourth of July
At the Franklin Savings Bank, NYC

Faces as anxious,
Bodies as thick and restless,
One black long-legged sixteenyearold sways,
One small child fretting;
White-haired, immediately ahead,
She talks talks talks to
(Thank god not to me)
Her unwilling scrawny neighbour:
"In the same building over thirty years
　Her son owns that dress-store across the street, *Glora Lee*,
　How she always gives the super two dollars when he comes around
　He deserves it but those others"
　　(Poking the laconic elbow next her)
"Oh of course some of them are decent
　And she had one cleaning-woman for years
　Who came to the son's Bar-Mitzvah (your Confirmation you know)
　and to his wedding"

Keeping what gap one can,
Goes out through my eyeballs this city's essential stare
Raking these all and sundry,
That bag-eyed old kitten under her jetty hair,
The slouch-bellied Germanic type where the line bends,
The housewifely bottom in the pea-green slacks.

In former years
There were charms against such days,
Hail Mary, Our Father, repeated
In penance, suing for grace
But now
One cannot flap dead prayers around any more.

At least let me work here
To feelingly watch
The thirty-two knots of pain
Ahead of me to the money counter.

Mother Church

The eyes are swallowed up in fat

When we go to visit
The mind seems vacuity,
Knows nothing of our real lives
Or even that we have such

The hands have not prepared any food for us
Lo these many years

The voice, unrecognizable
Between raucous and ingratiating,
Tells us to be moral
Or, repeatedly, asks us for money

Remember the age and deafness,
Remember the long history of anxiety neurosis,
Lest you burst with this warring heartful
Of fury and compassion and pain

Though we cannot for ever
Wheel the chair so that the face is in the sun
And answer those banalities
With careful nothings from our own mouths

We siblings cling together,
Try to support one another, to feed, sustain,
To love,
And speak now very bluntly as one does in such cases,
Saying, "Since this is how things are,
The sooner it is over the better."

Among Charismatics

In churchrows we sit as,
Kind minister murmuring,
She speaks of Silence
When suddenly stands behind me
Silence, bends over my right shoulder
To lay cheek to my right cheek,
O long strength of jaw-line,
Sweet heavy head.

If right side lose its hearing,
Leaned onto Silence' left
(Thus father, sister, genes ago)
Deaf skull need know: only this other,
Down whose far watershed
Ebullient hair tumbles.

In today's rivulet of cajoling speech,
At an ear half-closed, bone confirms bone,
Strange loved presence
And no word said.

"War and Hunting"
Reading *Vala or the Four Zoas* in the dog-days

    William Blake will go hunting in Heaven
        this tideless morning;
    Who will he go after? –
        as he takes out his flaming spears
        stacked in the golden umbrella-stand
        behind the door

    He will go after Nicholas of Cusa
        at the place where two ends cross
        where hot fizzes upon cold
        red upon green
        error upon revelation

    Or he is after Swedenborg
        who lumbers in a huge painted coach across sultry desarts
        looking out the window
        while Blake rages behind,
        lightning sparkles issuing from his red hair,
        & brandishes his arms

    Will there not be fallings-out into the abyss,
        as Eternals plunge headlong
        to disturb the great sea-serpent,
        untold groans, earthquakes,
        rivers of blood? –

    Till Catherine Blake
        in her embroidered cotton apron
        walks to the orchard path
        and calls under the fruiting apple boughs:
        "Mr. Blake, it is time for your elevenses."

          Eye of a Peacock's Tail, *cauda pavonis*
                in the alembic glass

     where Bubbles rise, take tincture, burst
             with a faint wetness, vibration of spume

      to tingle in the ear

as 'twere a Bell or Cannon heard behind a Hill
a Monochord sounding the notes on an eighth
                Pythagorean

                    till all dissolves to silence
                                    to nothing
                bodies changed to Light
                            as Nature conforms to herself

             water on which flies walk without wetting their feet

             small feathers falling in the open air

     PRINCIPIA is yet to write.   And read.

as above, so below —
        leaf gold ☉, massy gold ☉,

    Dust of the Road, Ashes, a Mouse's colour
    or that of the Nails on a Man's Hand

        Soot and Sea-salt ⊖, Rust ♂,

Orpiment, Cinnabar, Camphire and Balsam,
                all powders of the merchant,
    Linseed with Spirits of Turpentine and Amber,
        olfactory,
        Wax, Pitch, Tallow,
Wood when split the hue of a Man's Skin
Soap, Malt, Carraway seeds, Blood, minute corpuscles
                (as those of Light)

        sulphur 🜍, flaming Smoak

    hot Springs and burning Mountains
    causing the Land to slide and the Sea to boil

Earthquakes, Hurricanoes, mineral Coruscations in Earth's Pores,
                                            Earth's Bowels,
fiery and suffocating Exhalations pent in subterraneous Caverns
    explode, shoot heavenwards, vanish in Air and Vapour

        only to return as Meteor Showers, drops of Hail,
                                    Rainbows
which Monsieur Grimaldi may watch, cat-like, from his dry casement,
and Monsieur Des Cartes (at his sleight of hand?)
        but we will baffle the monsieurs

        ignis fatuus and now to be extinguished
        in stagnating Water

        and diving deep into the Sea
        become fluid and globular Parcels

the Light trembling and short and swift

 broken bits of Mirror
the backs quicksilver'd o'er with the bright cast of joy
are set in Water

      green-making
      yellow-making   Rays
      orange-making

Lavender, Rue and Marjoram distilled to
Oil, clear Oil, of Clove, Orange, Olives,

    pseudo-topaz, ultramarine

excellent Blue of a bright Sky-colour

gold ☉ and silver ☽, the ordinary green of grass,

    full bright purple, deepest violet,
    a violet more bright and fiery,
the colour of Violets is of the third, best, Order
    indigo manifestly less resplendent

and at the last, red of a Damask Rose
    sweet enough to drown the sense and make
    the Frame of Nature languish

as below, so above —

  to sail with him down Coasts of Refraction
where the Satellites of Jupiter ♃ waver in eclipse
    past limbs of circles
      of metals
      of the Sun ☉
who continues violently hot and lucid and warms the whole
          Earth with his Light

edge of black Riband fringed out into colours,
five clear, lineaments of a sixth and seventh

looking at the Sun ☉ through a Feather

pressing his Eye, that ubiquitous iris (of what colour?)
to conjure swimming mists, dark grey and russet,
from under closed lids, and now appear
deep dark red, willow green

working at times with a Candle, which hath a Ring or Halo

thus, too, great Sun ☉ and Moon ☽
have on occasion Crowns about them,
not least in icy weather:

other concentred Rings require
more curious observing:
and at the Centre of some, a black Spot
and of some, a white Spot

describing a burning Coal gyrated nimbly in the Air
describing fiery circles
(has he then an helper in the darkness here, apprentice
as in his furnace work?)
and pinched firmly in good English fire-tongs

grinding Lenses on wetted copper ♀

solid bodies, opake and pellucid,
also Marble ground polite

thin Plates of Muscovy glass
effecting Fits of easie Transmission and easie Reflection

island Crystal, Crystal of the Rock,

Diamond into Prism

Newton's OPTICKS

the chamber is enchanted

darken'd more carefully, opake the window-shut,
is this not he, the inner head, subdued, *camera obscura*,
into which through pinpricks in black shade,
    rays of godlight enter
    and something casts lion-shadows, mane and claw,
    tanquam ex ungue leonem ♌ on faint white wall-surface

we see him scarce at all;

yet active: piercing, grinding, painting,

    pinpoints through sheets of lead ♄
      (lead ♄ from church roof is best or the veins of stained glass)
    a pair of sharp Knives stuck into a Board,
    their angular shadows bisect for his calculation

he is painting the Floor, thickly, with grey Paint he has mixed

twining Threads of black Silk round a flat Stick

    now a Comb in his hand, between whose severall Teeth
    filaments of split Light array themselves

holding a Hair to aperture-slit
    to watch its multiplied Shadow thrown
      (where 'tis thin, where 'tis thicker)
    on a Sheet of white Paper

    Webs of some Spiders

♂ iron Wire

    watered Silk

His and her voice audibly different,
Gliding off, white throat gleams, fierce glutt
    For the tiny things that scuttle and cower
    In sand and succulent,
        So short a day,
    As blazes the evening star,
Gilt rim of new moon cups
Its dark bubble-globe, gold-dust besprinkled,
    Against the gathering blue

No images of closure,
    How glean
What is: to live, to die,
How gain some grace or wisdom,
        Small shower of pebbles down the slope,
        Glint of bees, laden, cresting the wind,
        One dry leaf glows,
    Signs, omens everywhere,
Goodly amenity, while we meantime
    Give them no glance,
How guess their longlost greeting,
Have we, in grasp, in innermost,

    No images of closure?

Meditation above Los Angeles

No images of closure

Look into this green grove
Brief glen, eucalyptus, what else,
Ivy-grounded, fifteen feet across,
    On a nameless hillside
Over the Gog-grown gangrened gorgeous city
    Between where the Pacific
    In a soft surf hem
        Stops
And the mountains, carved, wrinkle-skinned, sliding,
    Yield

No images of closure
    Do we have

Wild garden, where the deer graze
Unseen, thud and jostle, startle the sleeper
    By starfall,
Which now first daylight wakes
    To breezeless anonymity,
Circle upgrown that guards
    The abiding nest in squat thorn-tree
    Bluejay brooded last summer,
And gazed into the grove
    And out over the valley
        And gone now

No images of closure
    How shall we gauge

Yesterday's pair, great owls gurgling high overhead
    On cornice and branch, respectively,

Where we might have walked, younger and older,
Reclined on stinging dunes, spoken of wisdom,
Learned grace and symmetry from shells,
Danced ritual figures as the tide went out,
Laughed, wept, listened to one another
And the far singing cry of great winds rejoicing
In high passage through the air?

I say, over and over,
    perhaps not there those things we are to learn
  thus adrift
And where to —

So be it

Stars
    as solitary
    in that brimming deep
    of utter cosmos

        Stars
        you burning spirits

            Stars be our sea-mark

Teaching Again. New York. Hunter College.

Strange
there is no memory of some disaster
that brought us to this case

Afloat upon a sea of chaos
lumpish waves lukewarm
slap at us, shouldering us apart
endless, aimlessly

There are a hundred heads here
bobbing – visible
the few times the watery plain settles,
young males fringed and bearded,
seal-heads, sea-lion mouths,
and the girls drowning mermaids,
slight faces peering through
the black straight fall of hair

We surge with the waters, vanish, lost,
days and weeks, return
as casually

Instruct –
a voice can barely hold

Most immediate
how to keep afloat, breathing,
stem ebbing body-warmth
(they have their own knacks of survival)
and I
can take no single head between my hands
and strain for shore
Shore – was there once a stretch of golden sand

a friend going on a journey

we have a mad woman here
mostly she is inoffensive
we keep her in the back room
the neighbours do not even guess she exists

only tonight after your message of departure came
she began to give trouble
it is the moon she says (the *moon?*)
and the wheeling earth and sky

this has happened, I admit, before
and she turns ungrateful
to providence and ourselves
but that we must expect

and tonight it is the moon, she says, the moon,
that she has endured so long the being too late
for those she loves, and now to time
comes space as well

and philosophers may say space and time are relative
no, they are absolute, absolute
she is weeping, her head crouched in the chair
we do not understand her

do not worry, I will be sure to lock the door
or else, moonlit and windy as it is,
she would start walking, were it three thousand miles,
to where you are

Where the apple-blossom nods through the window,
  And the spring comes?

                              Ellensburg, Washington

Early May, 1970. Jackson State. Kent State. Cambodia.

Best to kiss her a long goodbye now
  While she is sleeping.
Leave the gentle spirit be,
With, as you bend above her,
The poetic mouth murmuring oracles
  In dreams,
Something about God's grace, dew, the loving imagination,
  All night long.
Go very quietly. Mind the door.
Let her not hear.
She weeps so easily and uncontrollably
  Nowadays.

The land is full of rage and blindness and pain.
There is a war, here, in this land,
  That's certain.
Go out into the street,
Into the rising wind and the choking clouds of dust
  Alone — you will find your fellows —
Go with a quiet step
And an iron right-angle of the jaw set hard
  Against what may be to come,
With fear gone at last
  Since there is no hope either.

But ill betide you on your return,
  Should there be return,
If you have let the beloved languish,
Peak, pine, grow shrivelled to a hag,
Or run about in short coats, carrying on
  Like a petulant brat.
For where will God's grace, dew, fall
Without the poetic spirit, the loving mouth,
  Without woman,
The gentle imagination singing and dancing to herself
  In the empty, happy house,

Beatrice to Dante: by another hand

I send this word by night.
Times have changed, Dante; the lady in question
(Perhaps you know this?)
Beatrice is in exile now,
Cast out from whatever city,
Washed by a great river and rising golden,
Was once, if ever, hers.
Those who know her best —
Were you not one of them, Dante? —
Speak of her lost in the dark wood now
Of this world,
Beset there, not by amber-eyed beasts of prey,
But the softer, subtler
Purr and fur and fawning
Of confused self-pity and heart's appallingmost pain.

There is some message here and now
For you, Dante,
Be you man or shadow
And certes poet.
Could you not go to her in the dark wood now?
She needs translation, Dante,
That only to be obtained through love,
To some even slight, twilight, celestial place,
Misty towers by dawn, the jocund city,
Or image it as you will,
You knowing better,
Beatitude she cannot, despite her name, now
Win for herself,
And were hell to go through first,
She would accede, were it in your company,
For love too needs translating, they say now,
And heaven, Dante.
It is begged of you: set out.

The Recurring

So here again is the wall
Right across the road
And daubed on the bricks F O O L the one word
In an emphatic scrawl.

No matter what road I take
Will it always be there,
The block, the character, glaringly clear
Even to my eyes?

Perhaps when all's done
I shall set my back to it,
Sit down at the base of it, slack,
And scratch myself in the sun.

Resolution: Against Up-and-Down Metaphors

I will exercise my soul in lateral movements
Mark the flight of bee into honeyflower
Explore the aged plateaux and rock-tables   of this earth
Sense skein of mallard   cross-cloudwise going
And swan skimming blurred lake surface   at day's end
Defy gravity and levity   leaping sideways into snowdrifts
Hold food in the mouth a little longer
Pay heed to the extended melodic line
To cold *couches* of pine-smells   in the autumn air
Invent sesquipedalian alexandrines   to sweep the ears' long galleries
Acknowledge the horizon   with appropriate gestures
And, in special,   what comes so naturally,
Wide spread of welcoming arms

Poet

I am the great white two-horned rhinoceros of Lugubabwe
   "Formidable" they say of me
I make forays on my pounding feet out of the drygrass clearing
   Despite the weak eyes
A legend in my time

   At night when the moon hangs high
I lie stretched out upon the ground
The saliva runs out of my mouth
My tons of greywhite meat convulse, heave,
   In my den
   My formidable sleeping-place
Which the moon sees

Longlived but not forever
I, massif, incongruous
   In these wastes
Look to founder shortly into white
Horns, white bones, heaps
   Moon-glazed
   In Lugubabwe.

. . . with new acquist
Of true experience . . .

Three from Boccea, Italy	54
Kind	58
Circle/Net	59
Runes	61
Figures on a Magical Ground	62
For Giordano Bruno. February 17th	63
Of Power	64
For Giambattista Vico and the Others with Him	65
Thurs-day	66
To Accompany a Proposal for a Conference	67
Danforth Conference. Zion, Illinois	68
Humanities Conference, Columbia University	73
At a Conference of Humanistic Psychologists	74
Lines to a Large Sculptured Head in a University Library	75
For a Friend's Forthcoming Marriage	76
Maybug in the Cotswolds	77
Prayer for a Friend's House	79
Our Culture Compared to a Glass of Champagne	81

Contents

Poet	1
Resolution: Against Up-and-Down Metaphors	2
The Recurring	3
Beatrice to Dante: by another hand	4
Early May, 1970. Jackson State. Kent State. Cambodia	5
a friend going on a journey	7
Teaching Again. New York. Hunter College.	8
Meditation above Los Angeles	10
Newton's OPTICKS	12
"War and Hunting": Reading *Vala or the Four Zoas* in the dog-days	17
Among Charismatics	18
Mother Church	19
Watching New York	20
Mississippi Revisited	21
Chance Meeting, Airport Motel Restaurant	23
Late Summer	24
Rilke: the poem inscribed on his grave	25
Song of the Fates from Goethe's *Iphigenie*	26
From Hölderlin's fragment, *The Fire from Heaven*	28
The Good Day	30
The Small Hours	31
How, for love, no poem will do	32
A Figure: for the Making of Love	33
Cor ad Cor Loquitur	34
Discouragement	36
in answer to your letter	37
Separation. New Year Resolutions	40
Attack	41
Dream before Winter	42
More than One Thing	43
Charm against Anxiety	44
The Bensalem Poems	46

Acknowledgements

A number of the poems in this collection first appeared in the following magazines: *The Greensboro Sun, Guilford Review, International Poetry Review, River Styx* in the United States, and *The Antigonish Review* and MOSAIC: A Journal for the Comparative Study of Literature and Ideas, in Canada.

The Bensalem Poems first appeared in the *Journal of Applied Behavioral Science*, Volume 4, Number 3, published by JAI Press Inc., 1968.

"The Recurring", "*Au Bois Dormant*" and "Maybug in the Cotswolds" were first published in *More than Magnolias: new writing by women in the South*, 1978.

"For Giambattista Vico and the others with him" first appeared in *Giambattista Vico, An International Symposium (1969)*, Johns Hopkins University Press, Baltimore.

Grateful thanks are hereby tendered to the Editors and Publishers of the above, for permission to reprint.

Copyright © 1984 by Elizabeth Sewell

All rights reserved. No part of this book may be reproduced in any form or by any means without permission in writing from the publisher. For information address: The Acorn Press, 1318 Broad Street, Box 4007, Duke Station, Durham, North Carolina 27706.

ISBN: 0-89386-006-9 (cloth)
      0-89386-007-7 (paper)

Library of Congress Catalog Card Number: 82-83593

Printed in the United States of America.

ACQUIST

Elizabeth Sewell

The Acorn Press
Durham, North Carolina

Works by Elizabeth Sewell

Criticism

The Structure of Poetry. London: Routledge & Kegan Paul, 1951 (Reprinted 1963).
Paul Valéry: The Mind in the Mirror. Cambridge, England: Bowes & Bowes; New Haven: Yale University Press, 1952.
The Field of Nonsense: A Study of Edward Lear and Lewis Carroll. London: Chatto & Windus, 1952.
The Orphic Voice: Poetry and Natural History. London: Routledge & Kegan Paul; New Haven: Yale University Press, 1960 (Reissued as Harper Torchbook, 1972).
The Human Metaphor. Notre Dame: University of Notre Dame Press, 1964.

Fiction

The Dividing of Time. New York: Doubleday; London: Chatto & Windus, 1951.
The Singular Hope. London: Chatto & Windus, 1955.
Now Bless Thyself. New York: Doubleday, 1962.

Poetry

Poems, 1947-1961. Chapel Hill: University of North Carolina Press, 1962.
Signs and Cities. Chapel Hill: University of North Carolina Press, 1968.

Essays

To Be a True Poem. Winston-Salem, N.C.: Hunter Publishing Company, 1979.

Memoirs

An Idea. Macon, Georgia: Mercer University Press, 1983.

Acquist